Praise for **9 LITTLE WORDS TO CHANGE YOUR RESULTS**

"This little book has the big ideas and essential tools to get you out of your own way and achieve success. Don't miss this opportunity to make life and work get easier." - Mary Morrissey

*"Remove your blocks to a joy-filled life.
An easy, powerful read which offers you to trade in your unhealed history in exchange for unlimited happiness. This will be a turning point for you"*
- Rev. Susan EngPoole, Senior Minister Emeritus, Unity of Louisville

"Make a choice, take a chance and enjoy the change. The way is clear and the way is outlined here."
- Rev. Martha Creek

Praise for **9 LITTLE WORDS TO CHANGE YOUR RESULTS**

"Lin's book is a powerful tool to help you achieve the success you desire." - Daniel D. Matthews, Speaking U.com, Award Winning Speaker & Certified World Class Speaking Coach

"Don't add this book to your book shelf – read and apply it instead."
- Dr. Brian Daly, Webster University Graduate School

"Lin Schussler-Williams shares with us wisdom born of experience and exceptional clarity. This book is one that will be read again and again- if you're smart!" - Larry Watson, Coach and Author of ***Rough Pieces: The Treasure Map of a Cancer Survivor's Journey***

Praise for **9 LITTLE WORDS TO CHANGE YOUR RESULTS**

"So many books promise solutions to change your results, but this book delivers! This little book makes a huge impact with tools to make big, positive changes in your work, your life, your world."
- Cathy Fyock, Your Possibility Partner and author of ***On Your Mark: From First Word to First Draft in Six Weeks***

Lin really makes you think about life, its purpose and potential, and how to replace bad habits with effective ones with the use of only 9 little words. Unfortunately, our brains need her remaining 11,600 words to get the point and then to do something about it. - Kyle Morey, happy husband, faithful father and the Chief Enthusiasm Officer (CEO) of the Madison Co. (IN) Chamber

Praise for **9 LITTLE WORDS TO CHANGE YOUR RESULTS**

"The 9 Little Words have not only transformed my life but the lives of my entire family - my son Tanner started cleaning his room regularly after reading this book! The concepts are simple to understand, easy to apply and provide amazing results when applied with persistence. I've shared them with world class athletes, top level executives, and children and seen all of them exceed their goals. No matter how much success you've achieved personally or professionally, this book will give you the simple tools for better results in business, relationships, health, or any aspect of your life. " - Timmer Halligan, Husband, Father, Author, Coach, Speaker, and Entrepreneur *(all of which I am better at because of Lin)*

"Little book...enormous impact! This book will support many in living their dreams... in living happy!" - Nancy Whitton

9 Little Words to Change Your Results

Releasing Old Patterns & Moving Forward with 3 Short Phrases

LIN SCHUSSLER-WILLIAMS

Copyright © 2014, 2016 Lin Schussler-Williams

All rights reserved.
No part of this book may be reproduced or transmitted in any form or by any means, electronic or mechanical, including photocopying, recording, or by any information storage and retrieval system, without written permission from the author.

ISBN 978-0-692-56325-0
Second Edition

Printed in the United States of America

Published and Printed by:

Enlighten Books, LLC
837 Cedar Bough Place
New Albany, Indiana 47150

www.enlightenbooks.com

Up Until Now...

I Am Willing...

No Matter What.

We must be willing
to let go
of the life we have planned,
so as to have
the life that is waiting for us.

— E. M. Forster

CONTENTS

How To Use This Book 1

CHAPTER 1

Do You Want To Change? No? Too Bad! 4

CHAPTER 2

What You Think Matters! 9

Take A Deep Breath And Read On, Difference Maker, Read On 12

Danger, Will Robinson 15

Holding Pattern 23

CHAPTER 3

The First 3 Little Words
– Interrupting The Pattern –
Cracking The Code 28

CHAPTER 3 (CONTINUED)

Cracking the Code 32

How Does This Work? 35

CHAPTER 4

THE SECOND PHRASE:
GET BUSY WITH IT! 44

The Brick Wall 51

To <u>Be</u> or Not To Be....What? 54

The Greatest Shifter of All 58

Flip Your Switch on Creativity 60

Creative Brainstorming 63

Speaking of "What Do I Do Now?" 71

CHAPTER 5

WONDER TWIN POWERS...ACTIVATE! THE LAST THREE LITTLE WORDS ROCK THIS! 74

Cut! 85

Advanced Decision Making 89

CHAPTER 6

GETTING TO CARNEGIE HALL – STORIES OF SUCCESS 97

James 98

Nancy 102

Janet 106

Villa 108

9 Little Words Worksheet 110

Endless Gratitude & Dedication 116

HOW TO USE THIS BOOK

This little book is meant to be a manual - an explanation of how to use *9 Little Words to Change Your Results.* These three short phrases will help you make a shift in your thinking and your experience.

Certainly feel free to read it cover to cover. There are exercises you may stop and think about along the way or come back to once you're done. Indeed, these are the types of exercises you may never be done needing and may find you want to find over and over. Therefore, the pages with exercises have a dark border in the middle to make them easy to find when you're flipping through the book.

In the back of the book are some fill-in-the-blank forms to help you, and they are available as a free download at www.IndieSalesCoach.com.

You will also find quotes sprinkled throughout designed to underscore the message.

These are also available in a document you can download at www.IndieSalesCoach.com.

*It is not fair to ask of others
what you are not willing
to do yourself.*

— Eleanor Roosevelt

CHAPTER 1

DO YOU WANT TO CHANGE? NO? TOO BAD!

It could be argued that since you are reading the first page of a book titled *9 Little Words to Change Your Results,* you must be at least a little curious about changing your status quo. The truth is, YOU HAVE NO CHOICE about change.

Life is change. If your heart is beating and you are breathing in and out, you are on a path of constant change that began, at least in this life, upon your exit from the womb. This constant change will end only when you cease the breathing-and-heart-beating part. In other words, the nature of life is change.

Your choice is more about the degree to which

you will play a conscious part in the change you experience. Will you aim for change by design or will you live by default?

Maybe you're aware of the inevitability of change and you would love to feel like your life is unfolding more along the way of your design than by random chance, but you have no idea how that works. Maybe you're like so many people who want to live more prosperous lives, and you've tried positive thinking or affirmations, only to find them hollow and insincere, or without result.

The thinking technology I call the ***Holding the Perfect Thought Process***, of which the ***9 Little Words to Change Your Results*** is a part, is a whole approach to designing and implementing the life you'll love living. I wrote this book first, rather than one on the entire ***Holding the Perfect Thought Process***, because I wanted to get something in your hands as fast as possible that could make a big difference. In my years of coaching and ministry work I have seen these **9 *Little Words*** have an immediate effect on people's lives. I wanted to write a book with immediate impact that could help propel you down the road to living life more fully engaged with your best self.

It won't take much of an investment on your part, either in time or money, to give the suggestions in this little book a try. What it will take is a decision on your part to follow what I suggest, so as to make the next big changes you face - whether you choose them or they choose you - easier to live through with more positive results.

As you will see, you will need to be a willing participant. No book or person can do the work for you.

Your transformation is yours to make - or not.

You must at least read the material, think about how it applies to you, and act on your new thoughts.

If you do, I promise you this: *a shift will occur that you will notice, and it will be a shift for the better.*

*Knowing is not enough;
we must apply.
Willing is not enough;
we must do.*

- Johann Wolfgang von Goethe

CHAPTER 2

WHAT YOU THINK MATTERS!

I bet you're thinking that dealing with the constant change of life sounds like a pretty tall order for *9 Little Words*. You're probably saying to yourself: if all those affirmations, visualizations, and positive thinking I've tried before haven't made a noticeable, sustainable shift in my life, what are *9 Little Words* going to do?

They will, if you decide to use them, rework the patterns of your thinking, your life, and your results!

Let me repeat that with appropriate emphasis so you can't possibly miss this point.

They WILL, definitely, IF YOU DECIDE with dedication and conviction to use the *9 Little Words*, CHANGE, SHIFT, and TRANSFORM

your old patterns of thinking and living. Furthermore, the practice of these *9 Little Words* will ESTABLISH NEW PATTERNS of living life full out, with complete confidence.

Are you ready to give *9 Little Words* a try?

If you're walking down the right path and you're willing to keep walking, eventually you'll make progress.

- Barack Obama

TAKE A DEEP BREATH AND READ ON, DIFFERENCE MAKER, READ ON...

The most astute reader - and I am sure you are one since you are still reading - will remember that I said these 9 Little Words will help you release and re-work old patterns in your thinking, in your life, and in your results. It is not an accident that thinking is first on that list.

In order to change patterns of your experience in life, in order to change your results, in order to change or create *anything*, the first thing you have to change is your thinking.

Neither you, nor any human being that has ever lived, has ever created anything without first imagining it. The chair you're likely sitting on, the light bulb in the nearest lamp, your clothes - they were all thoughts in someone's mind before they became physical realities.

Thought is the most fundamental element in the creative process. Without it, nothing is created.

*You must feed your mind
with reading material, thoughts,
and ideas that open you
to new possibilities.*

- Oprah Winfrey

DANGER, WILL ROBINSON...

In fact, right about now, there is a dangerous thought you just may be entertaining. It is so dangerous that it can completely undermine the power of the **9 Little Words to Change Your Results.**

I call it the *I Know That Syndrome* or the *That's Nothing New Malady*. If you have it, you may be thinking, *I know all about thoughts creating our reality; that's nothing new.*

Let's be clear - nothing in this book is new. Everything written here was learned from others - many others - psychologists, authors, speakers, teachers, ministers, and coaches, and, of course, my amazing parents (see the section called ***I Couldn't Have Done It Without You*** on page 128).

You have likely learned from some of them too.

But through inspiration and a perfect storm of influences and study, the myriad teachings began to come together in a new way, and one of the results was the ***9 Little Words***.

I had been a student of the work of many thought leaders for *years* without major results. I knew what I knew. I had faith in the goodness of the Universe. I expected miracles. I practiced positive self-talk. I taught others these things. I read lots of books. I prayed. I meditated. I listened to CDs in my car and MP3s on multiple devices. I *knew* the power of my thoughts over my experience and results. Yet I still questioned when this was going to start to produce results in my life. I often hated my job, and I knew my performance at work wasn't as good as it should have been given my skills and my education. I was frustrated.

It was when I finally stopped saying *"Yeah, yeah, I know this already"* and started instead to get curious about how I might hear it, see it, know it, or apply it *differently* that things started to shift.

So I am inviting you to get curious about what you *don't* know. What *can* you learn and experience in a *new* way?

I am inviting you to put aside *"Yeah, yeah, I know this already."* Instead, anytime you read something here - or anywhere for that matter - and you think, *"I know this," "this is old stuff"* or any version of that thought, tell yourself: *"there's more to know."* Open your mind, eyes, ears to connect with the more.

THIS IS SO IMPORTANT! It is your first opportunity to shift your old pattern of thought. *It is, perhaps, the shift without which none of the rest of the book will do you any good.*

So, mind open to new elements of old ideas, let's start...

Or let me say it another way, a way you have heard before, so get ready to practice...

YOUR THOUGHTS MATTER!

Furthermore...

It is not what happens to you, but what you *decide* to think about what happens, and what you make it *mean,* that is fundamental in shifting your results.

Again, there's a thought worth repeating with proper emphasis...

Thoughts become things.
Choose the good ones.

- Mike Dooley

It is not what happens to you, but what you *decide* to think about what happens, and what you make it *mean*, that is fundamental in shifting your results.

One example you might relate to:
It happened *to* me...

Many people walk around in what is commonly referred to as "victim mode." In fact, so many things in mass media, from advertising to television shows, are designed to keep us in "victim mode" that it is a wonder anyone escapes it on their own. The media reports the sensational with such relish, and this practice keeps us wondering when the unlikely will happen to us. I once read (I think from Alan Cohen) that if news outlets were only allowed to report on things to the degree to which they actually happened, we would almost never hear about murders.

Yet many people panic, mourn, and live in fear based on what they hear in the news. They make it mean that life, that is, bad things, are happening ***to*** me. Put another way, they focus on the danger in the Results, and live in fear and added stress, when there is clearly another choice.

Books have been written on releasing this *"life happens to me"* idea and replacing it with *"I can choose my response to life, no matter what happens."* Generally, understanding that I have a responsibility and degree of participation in all that happens in my life is empowering.

For now, I ask you to tuck this idea into the back of your mind to keep at the ready: the next time you think, *"I can't believe what happened to me today,"* you will pause and rephrase it to, *"I had an interesting experience today, and I haven't yet decided what it means to me."*

*Change your thoughts
and change your world.*

　　　　- Norman Vincent Peale

bitterness and revenge, he led his country to the possibility of peace.

What allowed him to emerge a leader for peace and possibility from a story of injustice, pain, and brutality was his thinking. His habit of thought, his paradigms, led him to seek the greater possibility for himself, his country, and the world.

This man's name was Nelson Mandela.

Now, you may have a story of unwanted pain and suffering that is more challenging than I could have ever known. (To read about my story of paradigm-making circumstances that I overcame, you'll have to read my book, ***Holding the Perfect Thought.***) Your story may rival the degree of hardship that Nelson Mandela survived. And like him, all of us get to make a choice about how we will frame up our experience and what we will make it mean.

If you have a story in your life that you have been telling yourself over and over, to the point that you cannot imagine how this story could be a force for good in your life, then these **9 Little Words** can help you - *if you will let them.*

If you are willing to break free of your holding pattern to create more and better results, you are about to be richly rewarded.

HOLDING PATTERN...

We call habits of thought that color our views of reality - like the belief *"the news accurately represents my world"* - **paradigms**. A paradigm is a model, a way of thinking about the world.

These are not fleeting thoughts like *"the kitchen table is brown."* They are thoughts we hold that become a filter through which we see the world and base our own actions. They may be thoughts we repeat over and over, or they may be ones we have never questioned and simply take for granted.

Albert Einstein told us we must choose whether we live in a malevolent or friendly universe. He was talking about exercising our mental faculty of Will to choose the paradigm through which we see the world.

It is at about this point that you are probably

thinking that I just don't understand the circumstances of *your* life. I must not know about all the things that have happened. Or you are thinking: what about all the bad things, truly awful things, that happen that prove this is not a friendly universe.

Let me tell you a little story that has inspired me for years. This is a story of a man who had every reason to believe the world was against him. This was a man who had been through experiences that had led many others throughout history to take up arms, go to war, kill or be killed in brutal conflict, or at the very least, seek revenge.

He was jailed for decades. His people were oppressed in their own country. He was helpless while his loved ones died, some in jail, others on the streets at the hands of their rulers. He was virtually a slave in a brutal mine; but instead of

*Don't wait for something
big to occur.
Start where you are...
with what you have,
and that will always lead you
into something greater.*
- Mary Morrissey

CHAPTER 3

THE FIRST 3 LITTLE WORDS. INTERRUPTING THE PATTERN CRACKING THE CODE

No change in your thinking or your results will happen without first breaking free of the habit of telling yourself your old stories. The first three-word phrase of the ***9 Little Words to Change Your Results*** have the power to do just that.

The need to effectively interrupt the old paradigm is fundamental to changing our results for the better. Remember, a paradigm is a filter through which we evaluate all our situations, circumstances, and experiences, and is therefore likely to have quite a hold on us.

Often these paradigms are developed through years of repeated experience. Therefore, positive thinking and affirmations alone are not enough to affect transformation.

Most people who have tried affirmations have had the experience of reading, saying, or writing the affirmative statement, followed immediately by a thought along the lines of, *"yeah, right,"* or *"Who am I kidding?"* or simply, *"That's not true."*

The truth is, your subconscious mind doesn't know the difference between fact and fiction. This is why, given a more fertile mental environment, affirmations can yield worthy results.

But if you think, *"that's nonsense"* and feel frustrated every time you affirm your new thought, you dilute any chance for real and lasting change. And should you do that—think, *"that's nonsense"* and feel frustrated every time you affirm your new thought—over and over, several times a day, for weeks on end, **what you create is more of you experiencing disbelief and frustration**. This is not, I am betting, what you were attempting to use affirmations to create.

Therefore, we must first interrupt the old pattern of thinking with a more effective tool.

We must dismantle the power of the old paradigm in a way we can believe.

Trust yourself.
Create the kind of self that you
will be happy to live
with all your life.
Make the most of yourself by
fanning the tiny,
inner sparks of possibility
into flames of achievement.
   - Golda Meir

CRACKING THE CODE...

The good news is that we have the power to interrupt the old pattern of thinking while implying the possibility of the new with three little words...

Up Until Now....

These words crack the code of **what has been** while tuning us in to **what will be** instead!

Part of the elegance and efficiency of this phrase is that it assists us in making a habit of noticing what we are noticing.

This may sound simple, but noticing what's going on within one's thoughts and habits is understood and practiced consistently by few. It is a habit worth cultivating as it brings us to a level of awareness from which we can truly change our Results.

The difference between applying "Up Until Now..." and simply using an affirmation statement is profound and important.

With this first little phrase we are not denying how things have been. With *"Up Until Now..."* we are acknowledging our past experience, and we therefore don't trigger the *"Yeah, right!"* or *"No way!"*

Because we now have the power to release the hold of the old pattern of thinking while opening up to the possibility of more, *it is crucial that we identify the parts of our lives where we have allowed our beliefs in limitations to limit our results.*

I told you at the beginning of this little book that putting these *9 Little Words* to work would not require a big investment of time or money from you, but that it will mean you are a willing participant. Here's where that comes in.

*"Forgive yourself
for your faults
and your mistakes
and move on."*

- Les Brown

HOW DOES THIS WORK?

When you say, for example, *"up until now, I have worried about money."* You are signaling your subconscious mind that the period of thinking that way is over, and, look out, here comes the new way.

So, how do you know when to use these words? **Apply *"Up Until Now..."* to any thought that is holding you back from your best.**

A brief, but by no means exhaustive, list of phrases you might use *"Up Until Now..."* with is below. Begin to notice when you catch yourself thinking thoughts that begin with one of these phrases, and begin to put *"Up Until Now..."* to work.

Up Until Now...

> I've been scared to...
>
> I have worried about...

I have always...

I haven't been able to...

I gave up...

I wasted time on...

I've been distracted by...

I've had trouble believing...

I've chosen partners who...

I have never finished...

I thought I wasn't worthy of...

Arguments make me shut down...

I always get anxious when...

I can't...   I never...

Try one out for yourself. Think of something you tell yourself. It doesn't have to be one from the list.

First write down your old statement on the line below, like this -

(Example:) I have always been scared to start my own business.

Now you try it: _____
_____
_____

Read it out loud. Notice how you feel when you read it. Now add *"Up until now..."* like this:

(Example:) Up until now I have always been scared to start my own business.

Your turn: Up until now
_____
_____
_____

Read it out loud. Notice how you feel when you read it.

Can you feel how these three little words take the power out of your old thought? Can you feel how they open you up to the possibility of something else, something better?

The energy of the old thought most likely felt constricted. The energy of the *"Up until now..."* statement should be more expansive.

Now think of something you have always dreamed of doing, having, or being. Write it down below. What else would be great? Fill in this blank in as many ways as you can think of.

Use your own paper if need be.

It would be amazing if...

Think in terms of every area of your life: mental, spiritual and physical well-being, time, money, relationships of all kinds, career, hobbies, and creative outlets. In each of these areas, what would it be great to have, be or do?

Now ask yourself why you haven't created that in your life. What is it you think about each of those things that is holding you back?

For each of your "It would be amazing if..." statements, fill in this blank:

I haven't ever done that because
_____
_____

or

I worry about that because
_____

(Example:) It would be great if I could turn my love of sewing into a career.

(Example:) I haven't done that because I always thought it was just an outdated hobby that no one would pay me for.

Let me share an example from my life we can follow not just through this first part of the process, but all the way through the *9 Little Words.*

At the time my eldest child became a senior in high school, we began looking at colleges. I started to have this sinking feeling about the cost of college. On top of the normal concerns about the cost of college, I had just walked away from a corporate job and a regular income, benefits, et cetera. My husband works for a non-profit, and we have three children, all of whom would now have tuition payments (our two younger ones have learning differences and attend a special school).

If I haven't given you a sense of the creeping panic I was feeling, just imagine me going on and on for a few more pages, which I could, and you'll begin to get a picture. I was truly worried. My college-bound daughter had some chronic physical challenges and specific educational goals, which meant we not only needed to find a way to pay for school, but it needed to be just the right situation, and darn close to free.

Are you sensing the creeping panic?

So, I began by saying:

Up until now, *I have worried about paying for college and my daughter having the freedom to choose the right school to meet her needs.*

Ahhh.... a breath. I realized I was no longer holding my breath! A space had opened up in me.

"Up until now..." shut down my worry and gave me another direction upon which to focus. But before I tell you the rest of that story, we need three more words.

It is not enough to understand,
or to see clearly.
The future will be shaped
in the arena of human activity,
by those willing to commit their
minds and their bodies to the task.

- Robert Kennedy

CHAPTER 4

THE SECOND PHRASE: GET BUSY WITH IT!

Now that we've cracked the code to our old pattern of thinking and signaled our brain that the days of the old paradigm are over, it is time for us to begin to fill that void left behind by the exit of the old.

The idea that the universe abhors a vacuum is often attributed to Aristotle, and in modern times is understood in terms of physics and gravity. For our purposes, the concept that where an empty space is created, it is naturally filled, reminds us that where we have opened room by releasing the old paradigm, we must consciously fill it in with a replacement habit of thought. Otherwise, a default setting of the former habit of thought will fill it for us.

In other words, if you create a space in your

world, be it mental, emotional, physical, or spiritual, you need to get busy filling it in with what you *do* want, or it will be filled in for you - usually from your default setting, also known as *more of the same.*

My friend Penny once went to a church service called a Burning Bowl Ceremony. It was designed to help release anything in our lives that was no longer serving our Highest Good. Penny was led through a meditation and guided to write down the thoughts, habits, and even relationships that she was ready to release from her life. Then she dropped her list into the flame of a candle in the middle of a big brass bowl and watched it transform into the energy of the fire.

As it turned out, this particular church had scheduled Affirmation Sunday for the following week, and did not include in the Burning Bowl ritual anything to fill the void left by its release.

My friend Penny did such a good job of releasing; she really cleaned house. At the end of the Burning Bowl Service she was glowing, happy, thrilled even.

But because she didn't get busy filling that void with what she *did* want, she had a week from hell, with all kinds of things she didn't want showing up. When I saw her at the beginning of Affirmation Sunday, she was a ball of tears, her head buried in her knees.

So we will not make that mistake by interrupting the old pattern, releasing it from our expectations and then going on without the requisite follow up. No.

We will use the second three-word phrase to affirm what we want in the most active way possible:

I am willing...

Now we will add action to affirmation. We will signal our subconscious mind that we are not just playing or wishing. We mean business!

In my example from my own life, adding *"I am willing..."* looked like this:

Up until now, I have worried about paying for college and my daughter having the freedom to choose the right school to meet her needs.

I am willing...

...to do my taxes early this year

...to learn about and file FAFSA in January

...to go to financial aid workshops with my daughter

...to learn all we can about the process

....to visit campuses with my daughter and support her in getting clear about what she wants and needs

...to be a partner, and to see my daughter and my husband as partners in this process

...to expect a fantastic outcome and be grateful for every resource and person who helps us

Now you should know: I really hate doing my taxes. I have an MBA, but the only C I got in graduate school was in finance or accounting. Maybe both; I'm not sure since I've tried to block all memory of either. So that may look like a no-brainer kind of list, but it was truly quite a stretch for me.

Writing that list did two things for me. First, it helped me get clear about what I *could* do to calm my worries. In other words, seeing the list in writing was empowering. No, I wasn't excited about everything on the list; in fact, it included some things I generally avoid until the last minute. But I also knew I could do it. All of it.

Secondly, writing the list allowed me to see those things I would normally avoid in the context of my daughter's opportunity for a school experience that could change her life for the better—an outcome I was dedicated to.

*"No amount of security
is worth the suffering
of a mediocre life chained
to a routine that has
killed your dreams."*

- Maya Mendoza

THE BRICK WALL

My coaching clients sometimes tell me it is at the point of adding *"I am willing..."* that they get stuck. It can be like running up to a brick wall with no easy route over or around in sight.

That's because often there are things you think you should put on that list for *"I am willing...",* maybe even feel you must, that you don't really long to do, like your taxes.

What you don't know yet is the power these three little words have to transform how you look at anything. Trust me, it felt like some sort of miracle to feel so great about doing the things on that list. I found I actually *wanted* to get to it!

I found, too, that what had been underlying my worry about paying for college was also a worry that I wouldn't be up to all those tasks and would fail in supporting my daughter and in being the great parent I wanted to be. Once I saw the list and affirmed my willingness to accomplish those things, my approach and my attitude were transformed.

The magic to transform our thinking is the words *"I am."* That phrase allows us to claim our power to *be* whatever follows it.

"I am willing..." shifts us from resistance to affirmative action.

*The person who goes farthest
is generally the one
who is willing to do and dare.
The sure-thing boat
never gets far from shore.*
                    - Dale Carnegie

TO BE OR NOT TO BE....
WHAT?

The clarity that I wanted to *be* a great parent for my daughter helped me to be willing to tackle any chore to get there. One technique to gain that kind of clarity is to put aside all you have to *do*, and think instead about what it is important for you to *be* in this situation.

You might take a blank sheet of paper and title it *"Today's To Be List"*. Then write down the qualities and ways of being you think are important for today. **This is a great exercise on any given day, by the way, and a wonderful practice to start the week or the month.**

Then ask yourself, if I am here to *be* this quality, what would I be willing to *do*? You will then have one item to go on your list following *"I am willing...."*

My *To Be List* from my college situation with my daughter looked like this:

I am here to be:

- *a parent she is proud of*

- *responsible*

- *loving*

- *supportive*

- *smart*

- *kind*

- *helpful*

- *honest*

- *loyal*

- *quick to get out of the way of her decisions*

- a good partner to my husband

- considerate

- a great example of how to tackle big stuff successfully and confidently

*Those that I admire and look up to
are mirrors
unto my own magnificence.*
> - Gary Simmons, Th. D.

THE GREATEST SHIFTER OF ALL...

If you are truly stuck on what you are willing to do, and the question of what you want to be isn't even enough, then concentrate on being one thing: grateful. Ask yourself, what quality would I be grateful for embodying in my *"Up Until Now..."* situation?

Now, if I were grateful for having shown up as that, what would I have done?

Now be willing to do that.

This is the shortest section in the book. Better re-read it.

*Gratitude makes sense
of our past,
brings peace for today,
and creates a vision for tomorrow.*
- Melody Beattie

FLIP YOUR SWITCH ON CREATIVITY...

Like flipping a light switch to gain the illuminating benefit of electricity, *"I am willing..."* turns on our innate power to transform our thinking and our actions. And just like the electricity is always there, waiting for you to flip the switch so it can flow to the light bulb, the power to choose is always available to you.

Often the way my clients are experiencing being "stuck" at this point stems from having thought about their situation in the same limiting way for so long that they are struggling to make *"I am willing..."* statements that break through the old limits. Sometimes the old thought that tells you, *"I can't do this"* is so strong that it strangles out any glimmer of a different idea.

If you hit that particular brick wall, then try

the following exercise to open a crack, or even a drive-through portal, to become willing to take affirmative action.

Success is consistently doing what you said you would do with clarity, focus, ease, and grace.
Success, seen this way, is an inside job. You don't compare yourself to anyone else. You don't even look at whether what you're doing is big or small. You look instead at the quality of your action and of your experience. Success is not about dragging yourself across the finish line or up the mountain.

— Maria Nemeth, PhD

CREATIVE BRAINSTORMING

We usually think of brainstorming as something done with a group or at least more than one person. You can do creative brainstorming by yourself with a writing utensil and a piece of paper.

You can also use Creative Brainstorming in a group. In fact, the entire *"9 Little Words"*™ process works to redefine a group consciousness as well. For now, let's stick to just you.

Here's how Creative Brainstorming works:

Number your piece of paper down the left side 1 - 20, and leave room for more than 20 in case you need it.

For this exercise, the only question you are going to ask yourself is *"What could I do?"* If other questions arise like, *"How would I ever do that?"* just set them aside for now. The same goes for evaluation thoughts like, *"I've tried that before and it didn't work."* We are not entertaining evaluations at this time. **We are only answering the question *"What <u>could</u> I do?"* Think possibility.**

Tell yourself you are likely to come up with ridiculous answers and answers you've tried before that failed, and *that's okay*. More than okay, ***it's to be expected!***

Once you write down an idea of what you *could* do next to the number 1, **do not judge it, analyze it, or question it**—*just keep moving down the list*.

Do not pause until the ideas stop flowing. Keep asking yourself, *"What <u>else</u> could I do?"* until you have at least 20 answers. Keep asking yourself, *"What's another way to think of this?"* If the ideas are still flowing freely when you get to 20 answers, keep writing.

Now, take a breath.

Look over your list and circle any ideas that stand out or catch your attention. Look for two or three that stand out. You'll know which ones need to go on your *"I am willing..."* list. Remember, it is okay to have ideas that seem ridiculous.

Here's a possible list from my situation with my daughter and college:

I could...

1. beg for mercy from the financial aid offices

2. do my taxes early

3. learn about the process and start early to take the pressure off

4. think, every day, "I can do this" and "we can do this"

5. Remember to empower my daughter and my husband and not try to shoulder everything myself

6. talk to everyone I know who has been through the college process

7. hire someone to help

8. go to workshops

9. listen carefully, take notes, learn

10. talk to people at the colleges not in the financial aid office for tips and to garner advocates within the system

11. pray

12. ask other people to pray

13. talk to other parents at visitor days to see what they have learned

14. read a book - is there a "Financial Aid for Dummies"?

15. talk with the high school counselor

16. ask my daughter to take a special get-ready-for-college class or workshop

17. find out what resources the state has that she might be eligible for

18. help my daughter research scholarships

19. encourage my daughter to apply for scholarships

20. get curious about the good that is coming from this challenge

Creative Brainstorming is a great tool for getting past "stuck" in any number of situations. You can apply this tool to everything from *"what do I do now?"* to how to overcoming what looks like an insurmountable challenge between you and your goal. In her life changing book, *Mastering Life's Energies*, Maria Nemeth, PhD suggests asking these two questions when one is feeling stuck or stumped in making a decision.

• *What is there for me to see about this situation that I may not be seeing yet?*

• *What is important or meaningful to me about this event or circumstance?*

She points out that these questions ask you to step back from your situation and act in the role of observer, something this Creative Brainstorming process allows for as well. She goes on to suggest that, after you have written your responses to the above questions, you step away from what you've written for even just an hour. When you return, she suggests the following, which is great advice for narrowing down of your Creative Brainstorming list:

Look for the presence of one or more of the following:

• *Words or phrases that give you a sense of breathing room or that speak to your heart*

• *An idea that gives you a sense of promise or possibility*

• *A changed perception of the dilemma itself*

• *Anything that prompts the sense that all is well.*

*Inspiration without action
is merely entertainment.*

- Mary Morrissey

SPEAKING OF "WHAT DO I DO NOW?..."

I said step two in the **9 Little Words** is about adding action to affirmation. So far, we haven't *done* anything.

Once you can see your *"Up until now..."* and you know what you are willing to do and think and be, it is time to take a look at that **"I am willing..."** list and ask one more question.

It is time to ask, *"What one thing will move me forward from where I am right now?"*

My coaching clients and attendees at my talks and workshops get used to hearing me say that the quality of our experiences is directly related to the quality of the questions we learn to ask ourselves ***and*** the quality of the actions we take as a result. So, let me pause just a moment to indicate that

this is a very important question. I know it seems normal and unassuming, but really pay attention to this question:

What one thing could I do to move ahead?

My very strong suggestion is that you make a ***habit*** of asking yourself this very important question on a regular basis.

*Faith is a knowledge
within the heart,
beyond the reach of proof.*
　　　　　- Khalil Gibran

CHAPTER 5

WONDER TWIN POWERS... ACTIVATE!

THE LAST THREE LITTLE WORDS ROCK THIS!

The final three words do not require anything from you other than your attention. ***"No Matter What"*** is a phrase that, when you mean it, activates your two twin powers: first, faith, or a willingness to believe in what you cannot see yet, and second, the Power of Decision.

Twin Power #1...

"No Matter What" reminds us to engage our faith so that we may expect what we cannot yet see. In this context we are not necessarily talking about religious faith, though if you have a religious faith it may enter into this practice perfectly well. Even without a religious context, we can practice faith in ourselves and in the universe to respond to our thoughts and actions.

So many books have been written about the impact our thoughts have on our experience of reality that it seems almost ridiculous to point out. The example that I think most of us can identify with is that upcoming trip to the dentist. Now, it doesn't take a guru or a neuroscientist to tell us that if we spend this week thinking, *"That appointment next week is going to be hell,"* it will be worse than if we focus on other things this week.

This is one of the ways the practice of that the **9 Little Words** can help us create more positive experiences—all the more so if we expect it to.

There are two ways to look at the use of this faculty I call *faith*, or the reliance on the unseen forces at work in our world.

The first way to look at it, and the one that most people probably think of as faith, has to do with one's relationship to the Power of Life Itself. Say you have a name for the Divine Creator of the Universe—God, Allah, Yahweh, Brahma—you pick for yourself. (For simplicity's sake, I will use the word God here to represent all of the names anyone has ever thought of for the Infinite Power.) Then you might find the connection to God in your life important by understanding that God created a universe for us to experience life in, a universe that reacts to our thoughts and prayers, and God created a way for us to create within that universe according to Laws that govern how things work. We were also given mental and spiritual faculties with which to figure all this out and experience it. Therefore, when your behavior (thoughts and actions) are in alignment with how things work in this Universe, the results are amazing.

To understand the second way to look at faith, it is important have a brief biology lesson. You have a portion of your brain referred to as the RAS or Reticular Activating System. It is located in the brain stem and has many varied functions. One group of functions is related to consciousness, and in particular it is thought to act as a filter to guard against overwhelm of outside stimuli.

Your subconscious mind can process up to forty billion bits of data per second. Your conscious mind, more like seven to fifteen bits (not billions, just bits). Your RAS pays attention to what you pay attention to, and then filters through the billions to give you the seven to fifteen tiny things you're looking for. But, if you have faith, and focus on the things you are interested in creating, you are more likely to connect with the resources you need to move forward.

The short of this is that, no matter how you

frame it - God or the part of your brain that sorts bits - if you are engaging in positive thoughts, emotions and actions, you can *expect* positive results.

In other words, it makes sense to have faith.

Twin Power #1....ACTIVATE!

*We all have dreams.
But in order to make dreams
come into reality, it takes
an awful lot of determination,
dedication, self-discipline,
and effort.*

> \- Jesse Owens

ON TO TWIN POWER #2...

On to Twin Power #2...

Bob Proctor has called decision a *"magic mental activity"* that can literally *"propel you toward success."*

A decision, it may surprise you to know, is something that requires a firm commitment, dedication, and an unwavering determination.

If you are feeling wishy-washy about something you thought you had decided, trust me, it was not a decision. **"No Matter What"** requires that same dedication and conviction from us.

The idea of what it means to decide has gotten watered down in our society.

A true decision is firm, involves dedication and conviction, and results in confidence.

Just to be sure you heard that, let's reiterate it another way...

Decision = Firm + Dedication + Conviction

Decision results in Confidence

It is in our moments of decision that our destiny is shaped.

- John Drennan

Now, understand please, the confidence that is a result of a firm decision does not guarantee how the decision will turn out. In fact, many decisions made by successful people are made in the face of utter uncertainty and great risk.

The confidence comes from the knowing that one will stay the course with the dedication of a firm decision.

If we are firm in our decision and dedicated to it, we can no longer suffer from the immobilization of doubt.

We will take confident action, knowing we are moving in the direction of the goal we have chosen.

I love tearing things out of the ground. I love digging and discarding. I love pruning. In fact, I love pruning so much that I once gave myself carpal-tunnel syndrome because I attacked a trumpet vine with so much dedication.

- Susan Orlean

CUT!

The root of the word *decide*, from the Latin, literally means reduce, cut, kill. A firm decision for one thing often means we cut away something else. If we decide for one option, we reduce the list of possibilities. If you decide to wear a white shirt today, you are cutting out the possibility of a blue shirt. The same is true in our decisions about life and our direction, and how we will experience our choices.

When we are changing our results, we know we can expect to encounter thoughts that hold us back and stand in our way. We know this because we identified them and used **"Up Until Now..."** to take away their power and interrupt our pattern of holding onto them.

In the example of my daughter and paying for college, I had to release the ideas that I couldn't possibly get my taxes done and manage all there was to learn about financial aid and FAFSA. It was the fact that the desired result of meeting my daughter's educational needs meant more to me than my fear or worry about it that allowed me to do it. I made a firm decision that carried me forward. The result was well worth the change.

We may also find there are relationships, or behaviors of our own within relationships, that we must cut away from our focus and attention in order to move forward. We may find we must cut away a job in order to become the entrepreneur we always dreamed of becoming.

A client of mine, Janet, felt she was meant to move away from being an employee and go back to being an entrepreneur, but her husband, who had lost his own employment, saw this move as too risky. He was clinically depressed and simply unable to be supportive of Janet's journey. She was faced with the dilemma of whether or not she could start a business while staying in her marriage. In the end, she decided to move forward without his support while doing her best to support him. Their relationship endured while her new business thrived.

Because Janet was able to be firm in her decision to detach from her husband's situation enough to focus on her own dream, both of them were served, as was their marriage in the long run. Janet's husband, Bill, has since launched his own company, inspired by Janet's willingness to interrupt old patterns, listen to her own guidance, and move forward with commitment.

Think of the problems you will eliminate by making many of the decisions you must make...well in advance.

- Bob Proctor

ADVANCED DECISION MAKING

If we go into a situation - for instance, a meeting at work - that has the potential to be tense, with the firm decision to remain calm and let nothing bother us, we have cut away the possibility that we might fly off the handle and scream at someone.

***Deciding in advance is
advanced decision making.***

When we decide in advance what we will think, say, or do, ***"No Matter What,"*** we eliminate unnecessary struggle.

When I was in my early 30's, I was seeing an allergist because I had been suffering for a number of years with seasonal, recurring sinus and upper respiratory infections. At the time, I was a two-pack-a-day smoker. During my appointment, he listened to my lungs and got a funny look on his face. He marched me back to a big machine for pulmonary function tests. A few minutes later, he showed me the results. He told me - with firmness and conviction - that I would either stop smoking now or resign myself to pulmonary disease, which was beginning already, but was still reversible if I stopped abusing my lungs with cigarette smoke.

In fairly short order, I made a decision to quit for good. At 10pm on March 30, 1993, I put down my last pack of cigarettes, and said, *"I have quit."*

I made a decision in advance of all the cravings, crankiness, temptations, and other consequences, that the quitting was complete, ***No Matter What.*** It didn't mean I didn't have cravings. It didn't mean I wasn't cranky as my body released the physical addiction (just ask my husband). But there was never a doubt about my response to the cravings.

❊❊❊ ❊❊❊ ❊❊❊

When I uttered those words, *"I have quit,"* I became the woman who will never smoke again.

That is what the Power of Decision can do for you. That is why it is worth it to decide in advance, ***"No Matter What."***

❊❊❊ ❊❊❊ ❊❊❊

Once you make a decision,
the universe conspires
to make it happen.
- Ralph Waldo Emerson

Making a decision in advance calls in the support of everything in your world if you are willing to get a little curious about how that could be so.

You may be scratching your head at that one, or thinking to yourself that I have gone off some deep end into woo-woo land, but the quote from Emerson above is just an expression of a phenomenon that is backed by the brain science of today.

Emerson could only have talked about this as experience in his day, but today we know that you have a part of your brain called the RAS (reticular activation system). I mentioned before how this part of the brain filters data. Guess how it does that? By taking clues from what you indicate is important by your focus and attention.

So, if you make a decision, in advance, *"No*

Matter What," and you keep reinforcing that decision with consistent, repeated thoughts, words and actions, your brain is literally designed to begin to show you evidence to support your decision.

It's the red Volvo phenomenon. We all know that if one day you happen to see a new model red car that you really like, all of a sudden they will be everywhere you go. Is it because there are more of them?

Maybe there are, and maybe there aren't, but you will be guaranteed to notice every one that comes within range now that you are interested in them.

Personally, I love the thought that a part of our brain is made to make this phenomenon happen. Given this knowledge, now we can know with great certainty, that to change our results, we need only to...

1. Change what we are telling ourselves,

2. Change what we are focusing on,

3. Get curious about what we do want and what we might do differently, and

4. Then make - and act on - firm decisions, ***No Matter What.***

Miracles come in moments.
Be ready and willing.
— Wayne Dyer

CHAPTER 6

GETTING TO CARNEGIE HALL – STORIES OF SUCCESS

We all know how to get to Carnegie Hall, right?

Practice, practice, practice.

This will need to be one of the things you are willing to do if you want to put the ***9 Little Words*** to work for you.

You see, our old paradigms are not just one old thought pattern, but a tangle of them at work within us. So, it is up to us to make pattern interruption and re-creation a habit we are willing to cultivate.

To help you recognize and think of some areas in your own life to tackle, first let me share some examples with you from other people's stories.

* JAMES *

Let's take James, for instance. James had a habit of raising his voice in stressful situations, at work and at home. There's a back story to how he developed that habit, but we aren't overly interested in that. This is, after all, a coaching exercise, and in coaching, we start where we are and look forward.

If you want to spend hours, weeks, or years examining your back story, try a good therapist. (Just to be clear, it is my personal experience that there are many situations in life for which therapy is indispensable.)

James was a small business owner and dreamed of having a business where employees were devoted, stayed committed, and loved to come to work. When things went wrong, he worried about being able to support his family and about letting down his employees and their families if the business failed. When the stress of all these pressures built up at work, he was known for his angry outbursts, and he hated how this had affected his relationships with his employees.

He was married with teenage kids, and he knew his temper had affected those relationships too.

James was aware he wanted to change, but the frustration or stress would hit, and he would blow up. So, he started with the first 3 words…

Up Until Now, *I lose my temper under stress or when frustrations at home or work get me scared about the worst that could happen.*

Because he felt he didn't know what he could do to change this, or he already would've done it, he sat down with his wife, Beth, and asked her to practice creative brainstorming with him about what he *could* do to help shift the situations and his reactions.

Beth helped him see that he was needlessly taking all the responsibility for the success of the business and the family on himself, and then letting the stress of that get to him and everyone else. So after he showed her his ***Up Until Now*** statement...

***Up Until Now**, I lose my temper under stress or when frustrations at home or work get me scared about the worst that could happen.*

...together they used creative brainstorming and came up with his ***I Am Willing*** List:

I Am Willing...

• To use creative brainstorming with my loyal employees to discover what we can do at work to better serve our clients

• To talk to Beth and the kids about ***9 Little Words to Change Your Results*** and ask them to help me remember *Up Until Now*.

• To come up with a "delegate it" list and create new responsibilities within the team at work and empower them to change what isn't working

• To invest in a staff retreat and some fun teambuilding to demonstrate my commitment

• To remind myself every morning that I am the man who is happy and grateful for all I do have—my company, my family, my opportunities...

No Matter What.

* NANCY *

Nancy Whitton was a coaching client of mine who went through a 12-week program designed to help her build her dreams and get out of her own way. One of her dreams was to write a book. She called me recently to say her book was done, and without my coaching program she felt she might not have ever written it. Not only that, but she included the following story about how the **9 Little Words to Change Your Results** had an impact on her.

I am so grateful for her permission to share this story here with you. (You can find this in Nancy's book, *Perspective! Shifting into the Reality of Love*.)

"When I was a little girl, I spent the night with my cousins. This was a real treat for me and my sister. I have no recollection of most of that experience, but I remember having cereal for breakfast the next

morning. After I ate all of my cornflakes, there was a pretty big bowl of milk left. My aunt asked me why I hadn't told her I didn't want that much milk. "Look what you've wasted," she snapped. I sat silently interpreting what happened to mean that I was wasteful! I placed that thought in a little corner of my mind and though that incident was long forgotten, unconsciously I played that self judgment out, in present time, through the years.

That was wasteful! I was wasteful! That was the thought I created from that experience. And, I believed it! When we identify with a thought (believe it) we're saying to ourselves, that's who I am - the girl who is wasteful. Then our minds go to work finding proof that this is so.

My point in sharing this story is that we don't have to let the past define who we are and how we will act in this present moment. We don't have to let a *situation or anyone define who we are. Who we are, has already been determined. We are made in the image and likeness of goodness and we can align our thoughts about ourselves with the goodness that we are at our core.*

If a thought doesn't align with the truth of who I am, I can change it. It could be helpful to change that thought! It could be fun to change that thought! Let's have some fun!

My dear friend and fabulous Coach Lin Schussler-Williams shared this 9 word, life changing process with me. It can help us lay down the dead weight of limited, fearful thinking.

Up until now, I thought I was wasteful if I did something for myself that I really wanted but went above and beyond my needs.

Now I am willing to see how valuable it is to

*listen and respond to the promptings of my heart. I allow **joy and wisdom** to inform my choices—no matter what.*

I am mindful of what I choose and appreciative of what I use.

I am willing to change my mind."

* JANET *

Janet was an accomplished woman who previously had a distinguished career as an entrepreneur, and who, when I met her, had a successful but unsatisfying role as a corporate employee.

When she came to me as a coaching client, she knew she wanted more, but she wasn't sure exactly what "more" was. First, she decided to move up in her organization and design a role for herself. But still, even as a C-level contributor in the organization, she was unfulfilled.

Once she realized she had a calling that included striking out in a business of her own, she then faced a spouse who was less than enthusiastic. Initially, she saw his objections to her entrepreneurial journey as absolute roadblocks.

We spoke recently about her journey, and she told me this is what she has come to realize:

Up until now I've allowed my life's decisions to be dictated by my husband's preferences. But now I am willing to boldly go forward, making my own decisions, No matter what.

Based on coming to this understanding, I have embarked on the career I love, and am not only having a ball, but enjoying more income. And, the interesting thing is that my husband is very happy now with my decision. He just wouldn't have chosen to embark on the self-employment journey because he felt it was too much risk.

By having this realization, I have written a new book, launched my new company, am making more money, and enjoying more happiness than I thought possible.

* VILLA *

In a span of three months, Villa lost her father who lived on the other side of the world, was laid off from a company where she had worked for 21 years, all while having been the major earner for her family. Villa told me recently, *"I could have curled into the corner in a fetal position, filled with self-pity, and mad at the world."* She didn't, though.

Villa is a great example of what one can do when a choice is made to live from the Power Within rather than giving your power to the circumstances and situations around you. Villa used the ***9 Little Words*** and what she learned in a coaching program with me to understand how she might have reacted before and how to choose to respond in a way that served her higher good.

Villa's ***9 Little Words*** went like this...

"Up until now I let my circumstances dictate how I feel; I am willing to let the power of gratitude, forgiveness, and imagination guide how I feel, no matter what."

She wrote to me recently and said this...

*"Your coaching program taught me to see beyond the circumstances and gave me the wisdom and courage to separate the Truth from fact. I am on my way to fulfilling my life calling, and my life is forever changed because of you and your **9 Little Words**."*

Thank you, Villa, for being willing to move beyond your old patterns and see beyond the circumstances as you live from the Truth Within.

9 LITTLE WORDS WORKSHEET

1. Fill in the blank with at least 3 things in your life TODAY that you wish you could create:

It would be great if: _____
_____.

It would be great if: _____
_____.

It would be great if: _____
_____.

2. Write a sentence about why you haven't created one of those already. Your sentence might start something like one of these two fill in the blanks:

I haven't done that because: _____
_____
_____
_____.

or

———— ❋❋❋ ❋❋❋ ❋❋❋ ————

I worry about that because: _____
_____
_____.

Here's an example from my life last year:

It would be great if:

<u>I could know I can send my daughter to the college of her choice without incurring ridiculous debt.</u>

I worry about that because:

<u>I don't understand the system and money is limited.</u>

3. What old thought patterns can you identify in your answers to number 2? Journal a little about what you think the limiting thoughts are that are stopping you from creating what you want.

_____
_____
_____
_____
_____

———— ❋❋❋ ❋❋❋ ❋❋❋ ————

_____
_____
_____
_____
_____
_____
_____

<u>Read</u> each limiting thought aloud. Can you feel the constricted energy - maybe a tightness in your gut or chest, when you say each one?

Now write ***"Up until now"*** in front of each statement and read it again.

Can you feel how relaxed the energy has become? What else do you notice?

5. Now think about one of those thoughts or situations. Ask yourself what qualities you would like to exhibit in that situation or area.

❋❋❋ ❋❋❋ ❋❋❋

In my example, I wanted to show up for my daughter as a responsible, helpful parent.

Write a list below in answer to this:

I am here to be...
_____
_____
_____
_____
_____
_____
_____
_____
_____

6. Based on who you want to show up as in this situation— that is, who you have said you want to be— how are you willing to act to get

your desired result? If you need to make a Creative Brainstorming List on the next page for ideas of what you COULD do, then transfer the ones you are willing to do here.

I am willing... _____
_____
_____
_____
_____
_____
_____

7. ***No Matter What.*** Period. Write a few sentences about what you will expect (affirm with faith) and how it feels to firmly decide ***No Matter What***. _____
_____
_____
_____

If you want to learn more about how Lin works with individuals and businesses, or if you'd like Lin to speak to your group, please visit www.IndieSalesCoach.com. You may also email Lin directly at Lin@IndieSalesCoach.com.

ENDLESS GRATITUDE & DEDICATION

My mother, Linda "Pokie" Bryan Williams, who died in 1998, was and continues to be a great inspiration to me. She was the matriarch of our family, a tireless servant of others' needs and dreams, a woman of wisdom, and a teacher by example. Even in leaving this life when and as she did, she taught me to accept reality as it is, to love endlessly, and to heal. I could not be more grateful to you, Mama.

My father, A. Dewey Williams, has always been a catalyst for my desire to accomplish more. He is an example to me of the power of having a willingness to learn, and he is the most generous supporter and cheerleader I could have ever dreamed of. He is the chairman of my Board of

Directors. I love and appreciate you, Dad.

My husband, Mike Schussler-Williams, along with my children, Morgan, Lydia, and Paul, have all supported me in my journey. I am infinitely grateful that I get to live this life with you guys as my family.

I am particularly grateful to all my clients for being partners in believing in the possibility of whatever I set my mind to and for showing me the results of staying true to the journey.

I want to honor and thank all of my colleagues and friends in LegalShield, especially the current and future members of Team UP and Success Partners International. They have taught me what it is like to work with an outstanding team of remarkable people!

I couldn't have done it without You...

My journey has included people from many walks of life. It occurs to me to list some of them by name, not only to acknowledge them as superior teachers, authors, speakers or coaches, but because the reader would surely find value in being exposed to their work directly should they desire to look them up. I could not possibly list everyone who has influenced my thinking, but notable on that list are these...

Maria Nemeth, Carolyn Myss, Wayne Dyer, Gay Hendricks, Mary Morrissey, Esther Hicks, Charles and Myrtle Filmore, Martha Creek, Bob Proctor, Price Pritchett, Larry Watson, John Drennan, Louise Hay, Gary Simmons, Cathy Fyock, Price Pritchett, Mark Leblanc, Napoleon Hill and again, certainly not least of all, my parents Linda and Dewey Williams.

Order additional copies for friends or colleagues directly from the publisher at:

www.enlightenbooks.com

or from:

www.amazon.com

You may reach the author at:

Lin@IndieSalesCoach.com

www.ingramcontent.com/pod-product-compliance
Lightning Source LLC
Chambersburg PA
CBHW072049290426
44110CB00014B/1605